Books by R. G. Vliet

POETRY
Events & Celebrations (1966)
The Man with the Black Mouth (1970)
Water and Stone (1980)

NOVELS
Rockspring (1974)
Solitudes (1977)

WATER
AND
STONE

Poems by
R.G. VLIET

RANDOM HOUSE
NEW YORK

WATER

AND

STONE

Copyright © 1957, 1960, 1961, 1963, 1965, 1967, 1970,
1971, 1972, 1973, 1974, 1979, 1980 by R. G. Vliet

Published in the United States by Random House, Inc., New York and
simultaneously in Canada by Random House of Canada, Limited, Toronto.

Most of these poems, some in slightly different form, originally appeared in:
*Beloit Poetry Journal, Blue Buildings, Counter/Measures, Epoch, Field, The
Hudson Review, Kayak, Massachusetts Review, The Mind's Eye, Minnesota
Review, New American Review, The Poetry Miscellany, Poetry Now, Prairie
Schooner, Southwest Review,* and *The Texas Quarterly.* "Mrs. McElroy,"
"Penny Ballad of Elvious Ricks" and "Jet Plane" appeared in *Poetry,*
copyright 1980 by the Modern Poetry Association.

*Grateful acknowledgment is made to the Vermont Council on the Arts for a
grant which helped me to complete this book, and to the following for
permission to reprint from previous collections:*

Kayak Books: Eight poems from *The Man with the Black Mouth.*

The Viking Press: Ten poems from *Events & Celebrations* by R. G. Vliet.
Copyright © 1966 by R. G. Vliet. Reprinted by permission of Viking
Penguin Inc.

Houghton Mifflin Company: Excerpt from *The Duino Elegies & Sonnets to
Orpheus* by Rainer Maria Rilke, translated by A. Poulin, Jr. Copyright ©
1975, 1976, 1977 by A. Poulin. Reprinted by permission of Houghton Mifflin
Company.

The Hudson Review: "Passage," reprinted by permission from *The Hudson
Review,* Volume XXXII, Number 4 (Winter, 1979/80). Copyright © 1979 by
R. G. Vliet.

Library of Congress Cataloging in Publication Data

Vliet, R G 1929–
Water and stone.

I. Title.
PS3543.L5w3   811'.5'4   79-5524
ISBN 0-394-50617-0
ISBN 0-394-73866-7 pbk.

Manufactured in the United States of America

98765432

FIRST EDITION

ANN

Maybe we're here only to say: house,
bridge, well, gate, jug, olive tree, window—
at most, pillar, tower . . . *but to say them, remember,*
oh, to say them in a way that the things themselves
never dreamed of existing so intensely.

—Rilke, *The Ninth Elegy*
(translation by A. Poulin, Jr.)

CONTENTS

I

ONEONTA, NEW YORK

The scraped sidewalks, the glazed
hardened snow. Someone
has flung a dime into the sky.
The college girls hurry
to classes, their skin smoking
inside their slips, dresses, sweaters,
coats. Cold tears
are at the edges of our eyes. Our hair
crackles with electric cold.
The naked, iron-torsoed
elms' roots go under
the sidewalks—how can they live
in those vaults? Our hands are deep
in the bear caves of our pockets.
They think of straw and dry
leaves. Our cheeks are rigid.
To move our jaws might make
them crack. We could be crushed
so easily by stone buildings.
To go into hot rooms
where there is coffee is not to go
into a true world. Our lenses
mist. We are strange
without our constricted hearts,
our overcoats. Here outside, the frame
houses are like Viking boats
caught in the floes, their lapstrakes
sheeted with ice. Our blood
huddles in our stomachs. Our pale

shadows die at four
o'clock.
          Right now I am in Mexico:
the Sun
hammers and brightens the leaves,
kindles the bituminous black
feathers of the ani, fattens
the mangoes, heats them to the seed.

EMILY DICKINSON

Who that life was
is clear: the wrist that moved
near the table, the white dress
in the shadow, sidestepping the square
sunlight on the floor lest it burn
the hem of it. Apples are pared
and notes sent and the black
stud is kept in the stable.
Fires light her pillow.
Morningtimes the garden smokes.
September. September. September.
Doors are kept ajar,
but only so. The circus is outside
the windows. The bread rises,
jelly is put in jars,
the hand is on the newel.
Shoes glide up the stairs
and the small attic burns.

THIS FACE

                the brow
drawn tight, the rough
hair. What time does,
you know. Cuts us back,
makes spare, pain
white as stripped bone.
Sunlight, sunlight, your face
moved from the doorway,
eyes blinking there, dear
being umbrella'd by childhood,
by our love words
too. Now we are shown
the white bone fingers.
Now we drink what
water comes through them.

THE PEACEABLE KINGDOM

A Primitive

Then men from their worn
dominions sleep—in the sham
robes, in the plundered gowns
shorn of sheep, torn
from the breasts of geese and hens—
under the high slain ram

and the moon that for them shows
a broken rabbit in its face.
It sheds cold light
through clouds sloughed as snow
down this October slant of night.
Then men sleep. Space

grows mineral and quiet. The tools
of theft and death hang
in the barns. Into the inhuman sweet
silence groundhogs and moles
ascend and feed. Rabbits
range for kernels along

the close-order fieldcorn rows
ranked tight as human
armies shining and metal-bladed,
plumed, marching to be mowed.
Beasts possess the field.
Mice climb the cane

spears and deer browse
on swords. And the first light
shall be the crowned cock's domain
who crows, the eastward-facing cows
and sheep lift their heads in plain
majesty by divine right.

BALLAD

His face was dark as Mexico
and gun blue was his hair
and he has cleared two acres of thorns
and one of prickly pear,
one of prickly pear.

The wife she stood by the kitchen shade
the rancher he stood at the door
"I've no use for you to finish my lots
and you owe me for beans and more,
you owe me for beans and more."

*

"Don't go today my husband dear
for to burn your pile of thorns
I dreamt I heard the cruelest song
from the dark side of the moon,
the dark side of the moon."

She had not sat from the locking of her doors
to combing back her yellow hair
when who should she see at her own window
watching her across his guitar,
watching her across his guitar?

She had not gone quite from the room
not quiteways down the stairs
when who should she see at the bottom of the steps
with catclaw and cedar in his hair,
catclaw and cedar in his hair?

"What O what do you want with me?
What do you follow me for?"
and she mounted brisk and she took three coins
and she flung them to the floor,
she flung them to the floor.

Then he took out his long penknife
he was fairly up the stairs
and he knifed her until her own heart's blood
ran down her milk white knees,
ran down her milk white knees.

      *

He has made across the yard
and across one stony acre
where greenly grows the live oak tree
and sweetly sings the mocker,
sweetly sings the mocker.

He leaned his back against the oak
he moaned above his guitar
it was the highest hour of day
but the brush smoke it climbed higher,
the brush smoke it climbed higher.

He sung *mejicano* until he heard at his back
the husband and five tall neighbors
and he rested there and he waited there
and sweetly sung the mocker,
greenly grew the live oak tree
and sweetly sung the mocker.

CUT A SWITCH

Though poetry
may be in other forms
it is likeliest here. Witch hazel
leaves on alternate sides
of the branch. Such delight!
Tick tick, run your hand
down this branch, wet
from last night. It tickles
the wrist. Strip off
the leaves and use it
for a switch—*how plain I am*
how plain I am, it sings.
Then it is simplest.
                    But Cuchulainn
runs out and hacks his broadsword
at the surf. Near The Wilderness
bluebellies cut the corns
from their toes, by campfire light.
The ship with black canvas
sails into Lincoln's brain.
Cut a switch. Here in Mexico
a speckled mango drops
outside our window. Beloved,
so many times
has your head lain on my arm,
the face so—
                    small
celebrations in their own right.

Swat the air. Limber
in fist lop flowers low.
Then poke it in the ground.
The switch will grow.

A PHOTOGRAPH

I

Backed by pasteboard and a warp of years
you seem a small girl proper to seminaries
you seem so straitly proportioned and your wrist
sustains so delicately the false fenceprop.

Our Dear Friend says: Hardly. You were big,
bigboned to follow behind an ox,
manly upon a horse, sheepfetcher, could heft
a rifle through the brush, girl the hounds
led, winter needlegrass and buffaloburrs
festering your skirt. Onetime you wore
a choker of red laurelbeans and acorns.

But now your skirt is stiff and formal
as leather, heavy with hips, this day
prodded from seminary: you are poised
as a lady: upheld in the stiff back, breasts
under white blouse spattered with Saturday
lace, a cameo like a seal at your neck.

II

What is real, this or that other
day outside this picture when you woke
the sister here beside me now
Goodmorning, went out to a sound
of hounds, to such circles of morning
light
        and found your self there
caught halfway through the wire,

13

the rifle hugged with sudden fact
to let a blunt tongued bullet
through your breast, your mouth pressing
kisses of dirt,
                    when your mother
rocked you in halfcircles of her distress
under a live oak and never spoke
and pinched ripe burrs from your dress?

   III
Doves in season fall.
Helped by ringtails black
persimmons fall, the call
of hounds drops ringtails:
October when red laurel
beans, acorns of live oak
fall. And the world is real.

For
Ramona McBryde
and
Lorita Gibbens McBryde

14

POEM

I

The mountain floats in the air.
The white horse under the mango trees
moves in the shade: he finds
a little grass among the weeds.
My hands are not quiet! not quiet!
and I cannot think.

II

First the women pulled the vines,
dry dirt in the roots,
then the bean beaters beat
the heaps, and the black beans
spilled like millet underneath.

III

Here is the rufous-crowned
sparrow, its breast like oatmeal.
It picks at the scales in the orange tree.
I wish I had those wings.

II

PASSAGE

PASSAGE

I

Out of the cracked ice, the blue
crevasse: I'm a polar pup on a drifting
floe.
       What is this light through drawn
brown shades?
              Bundled like a bear
and put to nap in the cold sun,
or with that little waddler my play-
mate in snowsuits and knitted scarfs
and mitts, tumbling on icy grass,
trying to twist our unlimber necks
like winter sparrows—across the street
the black box was brought down
the stairs, the wooden stairs, the stairs
with flaky gray paint.
                 Puddles
from wet arctics on a kitchen floor.

II

THE MINIÉ BALL

Scraped it up out of leaf mold
years ago, its shape retentive
in savagery, in rotted sticks and leaves.
Blunted tip, white jacket
of corrosion. Washed in the creek, cleaned
of its debris, it lay like a lead suppository

19

in a boy's hand. The
                      leaf-filled
                                  trenches
outside Alexandria. Beetles scurry
through the leaves, *tick tick*. A golden
turtle hisses, mound of hieroglyphs,
fat claws pinched between plastron
and carapace, a piece of bloody raspberry
in its beak. Here, wheeling the 12-pound
Napoleon into place—
                      a button drops
from the blue sleeve.

                      I think often
of them, with their lithe bones.

III

All night long, on that lava coast,
the suck and roar of the sea, on the other
side of the screen, boom and hiss
upward through spout holes: spray
on my thin blankets. Then, beneath sleep,
the blue moan of the desurgent demon,
shriek of stranded limpets and pooled
fishes. Mornings the reef rose,
a daily Atlantis, and the narrow lawn
was grizzled with salt rime. The night
mist dripped from the eaves. I ran
through the village with Sa'ii, under the milky
breadfruit trees, past the thatched *fales*
where the chiefs and their *siva* queens
still slept, huge brown larvae
in mosquito-net cocoons. The air
was smoky from the fires in *umus*. We stoned
breakfast crabs at the river's edge.
Out on the reef we watched women's fists
pull obstinate octopi out of holes.

Under the shelved coral, sea cucumbers
withered like wrinkled penises and squirted.
Schools of zebra fish darted
in the shoals. I built a boat
of tar and tin roofing. Myself
and a dozen other masters of the sea
rode the blue combers where they whistled
in through a break in the reef. Below,
the sunlight shifted from cobalt to green.
On the shore the white mission
stared. The green hills hovered around.
That was the sun of 1939.
One afternoon a German submarine
nosed into the bay, diesels muttering,
sailors crisp in their white uniforms.

IV

Genesis IV : 8

The flicker in the sourgum tree
at Cherry Point
has its eye on me. It circles
like a squirrel around the tree.
At Cherry Point soldiers with fat
(turtles down sand black with rotted
leaves scuttle for water,

               odor

of rotted leaves and tidal trash)
pockets on their pantslegs splash
to the beach. Rifles and netted helmets
rattle the holly

          at Cherry Point

at Cherry Point

        tap

           tap

tap tap tap.

                    I hid
all morning long in a pitchpine
tree, my hands black with resin,
chewing for thirst the bitter needles,
half in fear and half in dreaming
Gretchen with her knobby knees
peeing on pine needles, the down
on her arms, and her yellow hair.
Down below two men lay panting,
one in tears, throwing off their gear—
"will kill you" "no, I didn't—"
rolled in the hot red dirt.
One screamed. His face went white.
The other dug thumbs at his throat,
lifting and beating his head against a root
until the screams choked, then tottered up
kicked him in the ass. *"Next time
I'll kill you get the hell up."*
                              (Crushed
        holly
                crushed
                                        Field
*glasses and chrome antennae, quirt
and cowplop hat.*
                        sassafras.)
                        —The river
writhed in the heat, guns popped
around
                at Cherry
                        *"Get that
little bastard down from there!"*

        *

Movies were free and the camp commandant
issued the regulation Christmas parties.
My brother with the runny nose and close-
cropped hair followed me everywhere,
tick on my tail, until one day

    22

I led him deep in the woods to the six
Indian graves and left him there
beating on a tin drum *tap*
tap tap. He was shy as the strangest
stranger after that.
                              Circling on a mat,
coiled hair in their armpits, chins
dripping sweat, relique dogtags
jingling from their necks—
                              the fat
sergeant hollers. Those with knives attack.
Leverage applied to elbow and wrist,
backs slap onto the mat.

                              . . . rattle

the holly . . .

              White
                        rump, red
nape, yellow wing

                        —with
my BB gun I shot the—

hold the bloody mess in my hands.

      V
Twice I've been to the ocean.
                              In morning
light layered as mother-of-pearl
the blue heave hissed and broke,
littering the air. Lathered with foam
a green undertow
swept toward me and clearer fingers
pried sand from under my knees.
Curlews screamed overhead. Go
In, my father said. He wore

cap and jacket against the cold.
I balked and wept, my small
body summed up in nakedness, in elemental
fear, thin
arms drawn across my chest, blue
fingertips, blue penis the size
of a thimble. Spray laced my neck.

The second time a woman led me.
Under a stone sky, in emerald
air, no bird, no sound, no motion
but my own trembling:
love could have led me anywhere.
The pale, thin horizon was a ring
around us and ringed the dark sea.
We sat in weeds and sandburs
far up on the shore. You
were beautiful,
as you were meant to be, the small
oval face and slight body—
Ariel's spirit but Miranda's eyes.
No,
whatever you meant, the passion
was in me.
        A long, withdrawing roar,
mudflats and naked pilings: the huge
wave seismic out of Asia
blotted the horizon,
              grew in its
                  advance,
dragging the undertow,
             its soaring crest
whistling like the Erinyes.
            We
scrambled up the bluff. But I
as the curve lisped before annihilation
looked back into

my black soul terrible with power,
the god Eros singing in the sea.

VI

RUNNING, AND HOW I LEARNED TO FLY

Now, after surgeons' knives, cobalt's
basilisk stare, the destroyed blood,
I dream of running. Rounding the curve,
my breaths relaxed and fat, strength
gathering as it never does in fact,
once more I pull ahead of the runner
from Houston. I did one day
of crucifixive breath,
locked thighs and knotted back,
breaking through the wall of iron victory
into the arms, nearly, of death. But now
his is a complementary flesh, our pain
joint animal joy, motion
the very orison of being. I am
the god of the nine-foot stride.
                                        I learned
to fly of necessity. *Big ears!* they yelled
the first day I got on the school bus,
sandwich and two milk pennies
in my fist. Whereupon I climbed back
down, hiked my feet off the ground,
and in a comfortable sitting position
paddled my way to school. Got there first,
besides. From that it was an easy matter
to glide pterodactyl-like from roofs
and trees, then to grow feathers and fly.

I have come too close to the sun
of disease! I want
the joy of running, the quick foot,
blood taste in my mouth: resurrection's

hot flowers!
         Sleet ticks
on the window, and again I feel the nausea
lift its curdled head. Outside
in the dark the numb, bent trees
explode, shattering ice onto the crusted
snow. A gun cracks. In the green
heat of my sickness I run, this time
past dusty leaves, up an incline
on a dry, country road.

VII

Happy girl with the goldenrod hair.

Night cooled,
         pinching the air,
pinched a blood red moon
out of cap rock: the deer
were garnet-eyed.
        Sangre de Cristo.
Two granite backbones fell
to the desert sea, deliquescent valley
in between, and for three hundred miles
schools of mesas like lesser whales
hove from the swell. The first lights
blinked in Cimarron.

        "Those
    who are separated
        by a thousand miles
  share the same moon."

  *

In your dreams I am in the mountains.
The cabins have stone floors.
        Mountains
of loneliness, the summering Herefords, the fox
across the trail.

26

*

              We walk
by a river, under a later moon,
the ghostly sunfish hovering in the clear
water between weeds, a ghostly bird
piping its fear in a sycamore or cypress,
your hurt face laced
with cypress shadows
                              wild kisses
O my love
              I meant to shape
this poem compose it like a crystal
a garnet for your hair:

        your body has been my life.
          "My blood
        speaks to you in my veins."

Wet mouth
                clear-minded eyes
blue, with attitudes of gray
                                childishly
freckled face
                the breast I kiss
like a child, the other you offer me,
belly
        "milk white," white
as neck of 16th-century duchess,
wide hips coppery woman-hairs
lovely between thighs.
                        And you
have wished yourself more beautiful for me!

        *

But if ye saw that which no eyes
                        can see,
the inward beauty of her lively spright,
her shy joy delicate as her wrists,

    27

her strength to love welling like a river,
source inexplicable
                    shimmering with pebbles,
her calm mind but in her passions free,
her being grown from early grief
to natural tenderness, then would ye wonder.

      *

    This is the shirt
    my love has made for me,
    flowers on the collar
    and full sleeves:
    plain cloth
    smelling of midday sun,
    a few
    drops of rain on leaves.

   *

We both know our deaths. Don't grieve.
Through all time your body
will come to me, the blue eyes,
the quickening heart, the pain
of your dear words
                    voice
                         I hear
in the maelstrom.
                    Forgive me. I
was unworthy, beside your love
my own
the least stain of wetness under stone.

In Hell the mad, pure angels sing.

    When
   we shall not be
   may this song
    stonecrop
  flower of a small gift
   ever cherish thee.

VIII

The angel, unannounced, arrives. He is here.
Out of what sulfurous depth or center
of light I cannot know, or wait
to know: his first word is the poem.
It sticks to my tongue like a wafer,
transubstantial.
                        I drive up to a gate.
In the blood of everyday sacrifice a goat
hangs from a live oak. Flies
buzz. The sun pulses overhead.
A woman, whose hair is stringy gray
and face old, cleans the blade
on her apron. With her son we sit
to a dinner of fresh-killed meat,
biscuits and greens.
                        The angel knows
every sun in the Milky Way.
                                    A river
runs over rocks, clear, and a girl
bright-haired and naked moons
in it. Hoofs splash. she is taken up
into another language, another country.
And Soledad in her grief, and Reyes
come down to his death in a blue norther:
his face is the Mycenaean, hammered
tragic mask.
                        Behind drawn shades
day by day a quiet despair.
Sunlight on the square is cruel as Tophet.
The silent stars
do not touch our lives, they crown indifferently
the kiss under the lattice, the cries of Gutiérrez
burnt alive on a brush pile.
                                    O
be merciful beyond the brief
rain-lily, dark shade
of live oaks, moan of ground dove

29

in cedar, dear messenger.
                    I have made
this pipe of a goat's thigh bone
to play on, as I do now.

IX

Light spoke   opening like a door
opening like the roof of a house taken away
opening like the top of the night plucked
apart
        LIGHT
                    greater than the sun
or combustion of phosphorus
                            SPOKE
no other light than its own being
held
        then spread   exploding like a star
roots: lace: lace lightning: like
a net.

    And I saw all things:

those with whiskered snouts/ those
waxing into feathers on their wings/ tails
or no tails/ scaly/ furred
huddled in shells/ claw foot
hoof foot/ paddle foot
no feet/ those that roll into balls
that swim/ that crawl under rocks or are
the rocks themselves/ spin webs
sniff with ferny feelers/ creep
run/ crawl/ see or don't see
eat the fat of the sun or blood
or leaves or dung/ that sleep in nests
or shut their bone doors/ leaf out
by twos threes sixes nines
or sevens/ flower/ split from pods

30

crack their bellies/ make milk
breed in dust or ride the clouds
flat noses/ shovel mouths
that sprout branches from their heads
wear spines or are the true
jellies/ grow roots/ nets/ little
bulbed suns:

       and my own kind also
           thicker
    than leaves
those in death and in the deaths to come
   each
alone
    on the endless plain of time:
EACH ONCE ONCE ONLY.

I saw at a glance the pure
identity of each.

       The roothairs of light
touched
     all things, all things
blessed equally/ *linked by light.*
Containers of life now or to be
or long since put away

        were not ever
put away.   Each
was always the eternal being of itself

having once been, to be always

and the innumerable is
one.

X

AZRAEL

1

At first light,
the darkening hemlocks wet with mist:
annunciations of a wood thrush, water
from a thin-necked bottle. Always near
the ground, it recedes deeper in the woods,
from pubescent viburnum to mountain azalea.

2

We all live
in the same garden, the iris stalks
that squeaked when we pulled them,
the weighted brambles, our hands stained
by raspberries. Sunlight rustles the grass,
and the angel waits with his hands in his lap.

3

What is
this longing that always knew me? A window-
shade trembles. Joy was always
subtle, holding me unawares. Grief
was ecstasy—branch and leaf and the shadow
of leaves. From waste the star grew.

4

Het licht! ¡La luz! I'm a man of rags
sailing under rags coated with tar.

5

My heart,
accept this voyage: a new world
lies beyond. The trades lapse.
Strange birds are in the trees. Eyes
stare from behind salt weeds.
The language is silence, as yours must be.

III

LAKE ZEMPOALA

They are not happy that the people have come.
They trot up the creek and out onto the flat,
stepping on their shadows, black manes
and burnt umber, fat on mountain grass.

The red bus from the Colegio Guadalupe
commands the meadow. The people stand
in a ring, playing kickball. Sometimes
an Indian who sells bottled drinks
wanders up the canyon to spread
a burlap with white corn upon it.
In this way he is able to lay
a rope across the necks of two old mares
and lead them down to the children and nuns.

In the evening the people leave, their only message
paper plates and tin cans. Clouds catch
in the pine trees. The horses come down
onto the meadow. They step into the silence. Their hoofs
make no louder a sound than a pine cone
dropping does, or first raindrops
on dust, as they mouth the dampening grass.

SAMUEL PALMER

In this world there is no fear.
Such things as are scarred
are scarred to a purpose. The hare
where it walks knows the secret.
All is silent here.
The people waiting by the ripe corn
have eaten and are free.
Love rounds and plumps
every mountain and the trees
lift in ecstasy.
                    So did
the nurse stand by the window,
breasts and body lighted
by the moon, and the small boy
wild with comprehensive terror
receive the gift of joy.

THE SHADE

Light, and the sounds
in the kitchen, the quietness
in the wallboards. It is all
here. Sunlight
on walls and doors,
the breath of expectancy.
She sings in the kitchen.
I know what wet
aprons are:
I have risen through the floor.
I shall stand forever
by the stairpost here.
I have no other
desire. That is because
she sings, and the leaves
of the hydrangea at the window
are shouting in chorus.

AFTER THE LONE RANGER DIED

                                     they put him away in a cave.
For eight weeks Tonto carried the series.
Then the Masked Rider resurrected, a mite slower
than Jesus, perhaps, but just as reliable. The world
unloosed its bindings and straps and I slapped my horse's
rump through the sweet grass and the sour grass.
Such hoof poundings till my feet hurt.
I reared and neighed with the sweet iron bit
in my mouth. I was sexual and the sky burned blue. The white
light of a slake desert hurt my eyes.
I rode up the hill to the hanging tree and the bound
leather-skirted maiden until I was called in to dinner.

FOR SEX

I could go clear out of myself.
It lights a window in the thickening wood.
White grubs glow at its roots.
The poplar bends in the wind of it,
in wetness shining like a green sleeve.
When your face turns to me it is
your self, and more than the meaning of yourself.
Your body turning leads me
down birchbright corridors. Such a luminous waste.
The deer stare out of shimmering thickets,
the happy Chinese hermit dances
under the pines and in the streams trout
sing, we are such joyful commoners.

LEGEND

After the act, the three
slain brothers, the event
conceived in accident and error,
the chase, stone bridge
or market square, the pursued
caught, the smoking knife
and naked bone, the bloody,
folded clothes,
                        an immense
energy hangs suspended,
consummate, its motion no longer
forward, a stain in the air.

Students walk by with satchels.
Mothers push buggies. Cars
honk. A telephone crew
in an open, barricaded manhole
makes cable repairs. Merchants
hurry to their shops elsewhere.

A hydrant or a granite bank
corner, perhaps, but the blood
is under the pavement. Only the hulk
transcendent, the poise and the force,
defined by an ancient act
as light defines trees, causing
nothing, except to be here.

THE RITUAL

Why is it that I cannot
get out of my mind the ritual?
We have not completed the ritual,
whether it is candles or prayers
or simply a numbering one
two three until an end
is reached. I cannot sleep.
I place an object on this
or that side of the body,
a continual reordering of what
had not been done, and it is not
the right thing, it does not
stop the momentum. The propped
jaw, the forced-together
hands do not put a stop
to the pacing back and forth
behind it of my friend.
What is the ritual? How
can I acknowledge him?

SALVOS FOR ALBERTITO

They are burning the sugarcane.
The flames leap up like firestorms
on the sun, thunder of shook
sheets, the black smoke
boiling, whole campos blazing
and overshadowed. Four pairs
of tire-soled huaraches scrape
the road, flowers follow, the coffin
drifts on human shoulders
through the air. Tizne—black snow,
delicate carbonized fragments
of leaves—settles onto the long
blue box, onto our hair. They
have tied up the jaw of Albertito,
a kerchief binds his hands.
Nothing
will sing now in the capillaries.
His poor, slack legs, one foot
akilter, gauze in his mouth,
an eye part-closed: he will rise
like dough. He will rise
in his gauze crown and seer-
sucker coat.

        The bells toll.

Secret blood sprang in the night
between four candles,
an afterflow.

You who could hardly
stand pain, who said, "I would confess
under torture immediately," lay
two endless days, two endless
nights in an agony of flesh,
a siphon in your side, no plans
or codes to offer to governments
or God, your wrecked body
stumbling under its load
like a starved, beaten burro.
"Oh such fire!" and yet were patient
and gentle, laughed sometimes.
You climbed,
considerate to us who trail
behind, and when your eyes went blind
you worked as willfully and naturally
as a man with scythe or flail
alone in a field under the hot
sun, hurrying the seizures
until the blood broke.
                    Comb
the hair. Gather up the hands.
I dry the sweat from your face,
my friend, my kind, my human
self.
        The blue boat drifts
through the air, through the black snow.

Jacaranda.   Buganvilla.
Your hand above the chessboard;
the clatter of your typewriter, a box
of crackers close beside; evenings
on the pórtico: a kiss from Tana:
the creak of your wicker chair.
Flor de oro.   Tulipán.

I brush an ash from my sleeve.

The familiar face, the motionless
familiar hands
                below.

The Salvos

Sunlight on hands, on Tana's
face.

Fat raindrops
puncture the dust.

Here comes
the little blood angel,
mosquito, singing.

Night,
day's shadow: a wind rises
and mangoes drop.

Thick
horse lips: the white horse
strips leaves from the guamuchil branch.

Buganvilla, flowers like sex,
like scarlet tongues.

Voices
in doorways, in a room.

The dog
running celebrates its bones.

Brown moth, quick flakes
between leaves.

Male flesh
and female flesh, the slick

juncture hurtful and sweet.

Under an iron, smell of hot cloth.

Pavements brighten. Lightning
releases ozone.

Mornings
the eyelid lifts to light,
to birdnoise bubbling in the trees.

     *

Black grain is poured in a tube,
brown twisted paper, tied
to a reed: the reeds whistle,
rise: in the sky above your grave
explosions salute . . .

The cane will be crushed soon,
sweetness out of bone.

IN
MEMORY OF
ALBERT CROSS HICKS

IV

MUSCOVY DUCK

Thirty-six days, square
nestbox and yellow straw,
self-pluckings: Patience
with wings and shovel bill
pipes at Danger fetching
water and feed. Bag
of heat with erect, white
head, how can webs
and claws, legs scaly
as a turtle's, awkward and angular
as life, find a comfortable way
among the cue balls, ivory
ovals that darken with each
day? Breast wet,
she turns the latent images
underneath. The great yolk
of sun goes by, and nine
nights the eggshell moon.
Now these tappings
make her hunch up like a sick
rat. Below the hot cloud
of feathers hulls crack,
slipped cauls burst.
Strange, weak, reptilian
hatchlings happen under her,
wave their wet heads,
their little strings of gut
still caught in the shells.

PENNY BALLAD OF ELVIOUS RICKS

c. 1927

Elvious Ricks grew up in sunlight
and shade of a hackberry tree.
He ate his mama's spoonbread
and played on his daddy's knee.

Sometimes on the way to school
and sometimes in the night
Elvious saw a certain something
that gave him a terrible fright.

It was an angel singing
in a black-branched tree.
The angel said to Elvious,
"You must follow me."

Elvious went to high school.
He wore a black bow tie.
He parted his hair down the middle
and never thought to die.

The angel sat on the clock
of the Stockman's City Bank
where Elvious came to work
with his lunch in a sack.

The angel hovered by the steps
of the Ranchman's Family Hotel
when Elvious came from work
in time for the supper bell.

50

The sun went by high in the summers
and down low in the fall.
Elvious' hair grew thinner.
He slept with his face to the wall.

There's a girl in this story
with black, bobbed hair
wore a white dress to her graduation,
a white dress on her bier,

wore a white dress to the dance hall
down by the riverside
and to spark in her daddy's flivver
where she and Elvious died.

Her boyfriend caught them spooning
and shot them one dark night.
Elvious fell out of the left door.
Lorena fell out of the right.

They buried her in Comfort, Texas,
and Elvious in Privilege,
stone lamb over her grave,
stone angel over his.

IN A PHOTOGRAPH BY BRADY

I had never known
the art of truth until now
when I met you breathing
through the stain on Brady's photograph.
And I had seen the sleek mounts
with four hoofs spread
precisely upon the grass,
bell-buttoned general
squat athwart. I
had seen the squared-capped
private in Napoleonic pose
gracing the granitizing eye
peering from within its tent.

But while the three beside you
tower in sculpture heroically
carefully as in a child's game
of statues, you bend to the moment,
your worn back to Brady,
your fist in a caisson's mud,
your face forever from the future,
intent only on the present pain
and so, because you never needed
the camera's eye, alive.
It is the immortality
of this photograph that it, like art,
gives truth and being to him
who is not grasping for them.

Your hands (with hair
at the wrists through which the veins
plunge) are the only quick hands
of all that shaped the torn
cornfields, your back
the only back still
with blood to lift broken cities.

Breath is yours alone.

GAMES, HARD PRESS AND
BRUISE OF THE FLESH

boys banging one another, break and breathless
brush past arms, brash flagsnatcher!
Push, press, pound, pummel and pop
bodies, hearts thick in the birdchests.
Ache, squeeze, topple and tum-
ble tornshirted and kindercrazy, scramble and scratch
in the grass, bump bone and shoulder-scratch.
Smack, slap, swat, greenkneed, raw.
Nosewhacked breath faster and cold
shove! and then rip-out-ragged, knuckle, ankle,
stomach sucked tight on the run, balls
drawn up, trip, but though thump overhead
overheels, crumple safe at base. Spit, rise,
spout snot and tearstreakers, bloodyhot rage.
Rampage. Weep, holler, clobber them, clout,
snort triumph! trample, gag and rout.
Not flags of sex even can brag such sport.

TO DIE BY DAYLIGHT

is the worst terror.
In the sanatorio the child
is held on the enameled
table. Nurses cut
the green, wet gauze.
Me duele, me duele,
she cries in pulses
climactic, wellnigh sexual:
the putrefactic skin
hangs in rags. The doctor
sinks an injection in.
A señora bright-eyed
from fever, a campesino
with a broken foot wait
on a bench outside.
Sun lurches through a window.
Now it is quiet.
She lies
loose-necked, loose-limbed,
eyes part closed
as in death's noticias
while scissors trim.
Her breaths bubble.
I help the mother
to the market where
Nuestra Señora de Los Dolores
listens amongst candles.

Morir en el día
es el miedo más malo.

Today she smiles,
little Aztec on her straw
petate, bright cloth
in her braids, washed face
and borrowed clothes
and sticks for dolls,
and what died yesterday
only she knows.

ONE, TWO, THREE CAN GO

husband, wife and shadow.

GIRLS ON SADDLELESS HORSES

wool scarving their cheeks,
defy the glazed streets.
The wealthy heat of their bodies
(calyxed in sweaters and jackets)
thrives up from their horses
like forked slips and graftings.
The incontinent sap of their breaths
pokes stalks through the air.
Such crunch and alarum of ice!
and under cramped elms
what a procession of greenery.

MRS. McELROY

The front room was always closed:
the half-pulled
shades, the listening furniture, old
novels, Latin School Cicero, lace
tea-brown
curtains waiting in the still air.

In the parlor she put another chunk
in the cast-
iron stove, then sat in her rocker
with the tatted throw, among heaps
of *Christian*
Science Sentinels and *Monitors,* in company

with the pain in her hip, the constant witness
of pain
in her long hand bones: angels
of error she had daily to wrestle with.
She wore
white drawstring cap, long

blue cotton dress with flat
white
collar and white cuffs, black
apron. A cane hung from her chair.
I never saw
the ankles of her cricket-dark shoes.

Her husband had been translated years ago.
A rose-wreathed

saucer sat on the table beside me
with its twice-weekly offering of apple
brown
Betty. Before I split the kindling

we visited, she in the loneliness
of dwindling
time, I in the pain of a boy's
eternal present. The slop bucket
conjectured
by the kitchen door. Mrs. McElroy

hobbled through the yard, her cane
touching
this chore and that chore: slops
to be poured, mulch turned, thinning
of a strawberry
bed, tying up of brambles.

Under the mulberries, red stains
and bird
droppings. April, asparagus. Cuttings
of rhubarb thick as my wrist. Raspberries.
Loganberries.
In August I fought starlings for bushels

of bing cherries, fistfuls of damsons
for her tart
jellies. The sun still shines that shone
on her. Since then, my dear one, my mother
and my bride,
I have loved the struggling aged.

JET PLANE

Tail trailing like a ghostly pheasant's,
or
Phoîbos Charioteer:
smoke streaking off the axle.

V

WATER AND STONE

in the Nō form

WATER AND STONE

Nueces River, Texas. Early spring.

> *A screen with a rock painted on it, streamers of white water*

> CHORUS *enters, carrying branches of flowering redbud. They sit at each side of the playing area. Their dance movements are from the waist up, employing the flowering branches*

> *A* FLUTE PLAYER *and an* OBOE PLAYER *enter. They play*

CHORUS (*chants*)
We do not want spring. We do not
want these cracked buds, black
buds on leafless branches choking
with pink, flush with purple pink,
butterfly-crowd flowers.

> *They sing and dance*

We want
the dark to rise in the north, blue
norther smothering the sun, sleet
on stones, on bare branches untroubled

65

by growth. We want
                the silence of summer,
heat that stalls all breathing, stifled
cricket under the stone, stunned snake
and heavy bird.
                        We want October
when pods rattle, seeds drop,
branches scrape and the noise
of ripeness is so loud
you cannot hear
a man's gundeath cry
or a rabbit's screech.

Again and again and again. Sudden rain
lashes the ground. The river rises,
foams. Sap rises from the root,
hurting us with its power, hydraulic
power that crams the buds. Can you hear
the pain?
Can you hear the noise of the pain, pink
butterfly-crowd flowers?
                        Now it is time.
We do not want it to come.
We do not want it to come.
We do not want it to come.

                                    OBOE

Sunlight shapes the stone, the white,
changing water. Rain-lilies flood
the ground. The bird has come back
that comes back year after year
to stitch its nest of twigs. Feathery
sycamore seeds drop to the water.

                    FOUR PICNICKERS *enter, two*
                    women in summer white, two men
                    in sack coats and derby hats

1ST PICNICKER (Woman)
The river's so fast.

2ND PICNICKER (Man)
                The sun's so hot.

3RD PICNICKER (Woman)
The flowers are so white.

4TH PICNICKER (Man)
                The redbuds're so red.

                They spread a white picnic
                cloth, set a basket upon it
                and sit as if preparing to eat

                LEE BENBOW *enters. He wears*
                workman's clothes and a brown
                wool cap

CHORUS
Who is this man who stands by the river,
staring at the river? We have not seen
his kind before. All we have seen
are the two white dresses, the basket
and white cloth, the men in Sunday
suits and black, rounded hats.

LEE BENBOW (*to the audience*)
My name is Lee Benbow. I do my time
goosing a closed-cab truck. Down
from Brownwood with a load of oak posts
on my way to Crystal City. Brady,
Mason, Fredericksburg. West to Kerrville,
caliche road. Why do I leave
paved highway? Ingram, Mountain Home,
road built for a goat. Wet
creek crossings and twenty-seven gates.

   67

The Divide, sea of brush and flowers:
in the evening doves call.
                         Daylight.
I crank up the Ford, the exhaust
coughs and barks like a fox. Why
am I here, under this washed, bloodless sky?
Breaks of the Nueces. Take the old
Fort Concho Road south,
Joy Hollow, East Prong,
rocky track.
                    Brush scrapes the runningboard
here in the cedar-choked pasture where
armadillos snuffed among roots at dusk
and a boy lugged a birdgun after doves.

Canyon of redbuds. The river sounds.
The house is farther on, down below.

                    He sits near the screen

                                        FLUTE

It is all here. Nothing is changed.
Same light, circle of light,
every buzzing moment
caught in amber time,
father of leaves
and of the darkness under
leaves, when a boy was so close to the ground
he could taste the secrets of stones, talk
with a bug on a stalk, imagine dreams
of worts and fantastic lichens, find flaked
arrowheads. It is
the same sun
on bent, wet
weeds, drowned
roots of sycamores,

air stained
with mist, black
washed boulders,
the ropy falls,
hissing foam
violent and white,
the pigeon-colored water
broken, muscular—
deep,
below the rocks.

I haven't been here in twenty years. I said I'd
never come back.

O the redbuds! Pale
as a brother's drowned heart.

To the audience

I was eleven. My little brother Willy was younger
than me. We played together all the time. Once some
picnickers came to the Nueces River, above the house.
We saw them there. We asked our mother if we could go
up and fish and see who the people were. She said we
could.
We baited our hooks and began fishing from the big
rocks, where the water was deep and boiling up from the
falls.

1ST PICNICKER
Oh Frank, make those boys
go away.

2ND PICNICKER
        Even in the woods
it's cowplops and kids.

4TH PICNICKER
                    Don't pay
any attention to them.

3RD PICNICKER
                    I've got
an ant in my potato salad.

LEE BENBOW
    I had just turned away to bait my fishhook a second
time when I heard my little brother fall into the water.
Help. Help me. That's my brother.

3RD PICNICKER
Look! He's fallen in!

4TH PICNICKER
                        There
he is.

1ST PICNICKER
        There's his head.

LEE BENBOW
                    He can't
swim!

2ND PICNICKER
        Get back, girls. Get back.

                        The two men shoo the women
                        back from the scene

LEE BENBOW (*weeps*)
Oh god. Oh god. Please help me.

CHORUS
He could see his brother in the water,

70

head just under the foam. He
jumped in.

LEE BENBOW
        The water was over my head.
Willy grabbed me by the shoulder.

               He begins the DANCE OF DROWNING,
               accompanied by CHORUS, FLUTE
               and OBOE

CHORUS
The first
        rush
              of the water
                        is cold
mother catching you by the armpits.
Bubbles hiss through your hair.
Wet clothes climb like the web
of a water spider. Stone water
clogs your ears.
              The broken toe
kicks from the stone floor. Bodies
hit against rocks. What is this flesh?
Who is this stranger I am wrestling with,
water angel pure as an animal, who
grabs me
          by the shoulder,
                  winds
me with his legs,
             wraps me
in his wings of terror?
                The forehead clangs.
Asphyxia presses its tokens, binds
the chestband tighter and tighter—the huge
breath
STUNS the lungs, sucks in virgin
error. Light breaks behind the eyes.

Crawdad.
    Hellgrammite.
Stone doors open soundlessly
on their valves, down where the water king
lifts his weightless head.

LEE BENBOW
                            I tried
to swim under water with Willy toward
the bank. All at once he let go.

CHORUS
To crawl ashore is to begin the real
death.

                                    FLUTE:
                                    a redbird

LEE BENBOW (*on his knees, choking*)
            You can   save him   he isn't
dead   yet.

2ND PICNICKER
                    Let's get the hell
out of here.

1ST PICNICKER
                    My god, Frank. Do
something. I can't stand it.

LEE BENBOW
        I dived and dived for my brother, on account of I
knew I could save him even then if I could find him. But
I couldn't find him again.

FOUR PICNICKERS
It is the same sun,
the same leaping foam,

    72

black, washed boulders,
the same recurrent moment
eternal in horror.

FLUTE:
the redbird

3RD PICNICKER
                    I remember
the redbird, indifference incarnate.

LEE BENBOW
We sent for help when I got out.
Those men sent Charlie Ott to find
the body.

LEE BENBOW, FOUR PICNICKERS
          Which he did.

OBOE

LEE BENBOW
               To walk
is Hell. To walk on the earth is Hell.
Hell is to open the door
                    there where the sunlight
lies in a square on the floor. The smile
of the mother, the odor of baking
                         is death,
is to say death, spell death,
know death.

1ST PICNICKER (*screams*)
          Oh! I'm ill!

          She falls to the ground. A
          stir. The 2ND PICNICKER *helps*
          her to her feet

73

LEE BENBOW
They could have helped me but they didn't.
The water was over my head: it wasn't
over their heads. They could have reached
me a stick.
                    I never forgot
how those two men did. I said
when I got big enough I'd find
them and take it up with them.

                         He runs to them and tears the
                         cloth from their hands

Why didn't you help me?

4TH PICNICKER
                              It happened
so fast.

LEE BENBOW
                    Were you afraid you'd get wet?
Were you afraid you'd spoil your picnic?

2ND PICNICKER
I was afraid. But not of that.

LEE BENBOW
I'll kill you both. All my childhood
I spent wanting that. Diddling
over dinner, poking the tasteless food.
Drawing a bead on a squirrel. Above
a blurred book at a back desk
in school, imagining the pursuit, the confrontation,
the pleas. Climbing out of the suffocation
of a dream to stare at the silent movie
in the corner, your scared, comic faces.

74

2ND PICNICKER
I was in love. I was afraid
I'd make a fool of myself.

1ST PICNICKER
                              Oh Frank,
I detest you.

4TH PICNICKER
                    When I failed to act
on the first impulse, I couldn't act
at all.

3RD PICNICKER
            Such things don't happen
in daylight like that. It was a sweet
morning. We'd had a nice ride
up the canyon. The redbuds were so lovely.

4TH PICNICKER
Often in a doorway or on a street
corner—a slant of sunlight, remembrance
of water   I've felt the shame.

LEE BENBOW
                        I wish
you were dead, just like my brother is.

4TH PICNICKER
                                    Cross
the plowed field backside of Alta Springs.
Climb the hill of stony, yellow
ground and through a ragged barbed
wire fence. Over to the east
by three scrub cedars congested
with dark blue berries is where
my grave is. I came

by wagon through the stone-arched gate.
Eighteen years. The grave is as flat
as if it never had been dug.
                              What
is life but intensified emptiness? A child's
wide, staring eyes, drowned
face and wet limbs are the real
annunciation.
                    One evening I left my supper
on the stove, went out to the garage
and flung a rope over a two by eight.
The last thing I heard
was the chair hitting the floor
or maybe
that was my neckbone popping by my ear.

                    He picks up the picnic cloth,
                    folds it and goes off

1ST PICNICKER
Frank and I were engaged to be married
in three more months. After this
I hated him.

2ND PICNICKER
                    You broke off the engagement.
You wouldn't let me touch you. You never
spoke to me again.

1ST PICNICKER
                    I couldn't live
with a man like that.

2ND PICNICKER
                    I've been lost
in a funhouse ever since. Nothing's
real. Trees, people, buildings
          stand

into the air, solid as the Blarney stone
and just as remote. Even the ones
I love are strange,
                              stranger than most.
Had three sons by that girl
with dark, roving eyes
who drove her daddy's flivver,
who gave me the come-on
in the dance hall down by the river.
All grown now. Don't know
a one of them, her least of all.

Husband.   Father.   Deacon.   Rancher.
Last week I drowned at Truett's Crossing
trying to get a wagonload of wool
across the river.
                              That's a laugh.
Won't you speak to me even now?

1ST PICNICKER
I married and was happy, my husband
is a good man. My daughter
went to nursing school: she pricked
her finger on a septic needle
and died of lockjaw, shades
down and a terror of light.
My son had a wart on his ear.
It grew like Shakespeare's toad,
ugly and venomous, to be
a fat, precious cancer
gorging on the jewel in his head.
I go
to church to find what life
I can in the altar crumbs.

                    She and 2ND PICNICKER *go off*
                    in separate directions

77

3RD PICNICKER
It was a sweet
day, we'd had
a nice ride,
the redbuds
were so lovely.
Don't make me think
                    on ugly
things like that! The safest way
is not to know, or if you know
not to acknowledge it.
                    I never married.
I taught school for twenty years
and will for twenty years more.
I wish I were one of my children
standing on the schoolhouse steps,
washed faces, fresh shirts
and pinafores, waiting for the camera click
with wide, innocent stares.
Nights I dream of redbud pods
churning in the wind, hissing like foam:
Judas' face
                    purple on the tree.

                    She goes off

CHORUS (*sings*)
The trunk quakes, buds press
and crack
        pink on bare branches
petals litter the stones. The heart
grows pale, it beats and dissolves.

LEE BENBOW
Christ
        I'd pray
                    if it could change

anything! All our birthday candles
light the body on the slab.

To the audience

You and you and I
will go into suffering and death,
                              the crab
under the heart, the thickening node,
pinched breath, rheumatic bones,
the child in white in the box who ran
through this room and that room,
the collapse in the barn, the stroke alone
on the porch,
                    the phone call at midnight,
the telegram at work,
                         manic kisses,
useless tears,
                    stone hands,
closed face not even here.

*He falls to his knees and rocks
back and forth*

                    And not
to see, not to want to know
is the soonest death.

FLUTE:
the redbird

Silence: LEE BENBOW *looks up*

I forgive them.
I touch their faces, I bless their hands:
the white dresses,
                    picnic foolishness,

the sunlight and the fear. Let the light
shine down on every good and evil,
water, redbud and stone.
                    I forgive.
I drink the water. I kiss the stone.

                    He rises and starts off

CHORUS
It's not good to be human.
The blood's too warm.
There's too much in the head.
Even the horned toad
by the root, the lizard on the branch
cannot suffer anything
but the moment:
                    hunger, the sudden
shadow, unrealized death.

                    They dance and sing

To wear summer
in the leaves
and no other,
to poke winter
cold twigs
at the weather,
to appease the force in the root
with the brief pain of flowers,
to lift up and thrust
out and drop seeds
without love,
without hate,
without thought,
is elemental glory
                    endlessly
out of time.

Only *they*
know a night not an absence of light.
Only *they* ever die.

LEE BENBOW
                              Oh,
I'm so happy. So happy.

                    He goes off

                                        FLUTE
                                        and
                                        OBOE

                    The CHORUS *goes off*

                    FLUTE PLAYER *and* OBOE
                    PLAYER *go off*

                              For
                              Princess

VI

INVOCATION

Now
I know
what it is
to be
like the butcher
or
the hardware
man, my fingers
in blood
or sixpenny
nails,
the world
gone solid overnight,
practical,
a practical
misery, a pair
of coins
on my eyes,
my pockets
nestsful
of cancelled tickets.
Does that sound
like me?
I beg
You mercy,
mercy,
You
of the long black
hair
and the winter skin.

I have
served
          Thee.
This I wear
under my jacket now
is no
hunchback's hump,
but a blotch
of shriveled
wings.
          Come down
from the forthright
northern country.
Teach
me the true,
the harsh
necessity.
Strip
me
of error.
Widen my eyes.
Split my back open
like a late
dragonfly in summer thunder
uncrinkling
on the marshgrass
of everyday
surprise. I
labor now,
here.
          A wind
blows, dark
leaves
fly up,
lessening
the sun.
The room grows cold.

Ah!
        white
arms
            white
merciless
brow!

Judge me in Your severity.

POETRY (IF IT MUST COME)

must come never kept,
but unkempt and dragging weed
up from the seas, must be
bulbous-eyed from old
astonishments: a crank
species meant not actually
to be seen. Yet sweaty fishermen
hauling continually from need
sometimes fetch it up: it flops,
thumping the decks,
croaks—the fishermen
think they hear it speak.
More certainly it squeaks,
being slung in insubstantial air
and with all a dizzy ache
behind its gills. Its claws,
which must drip antique
moss, gesticulate: it knows
a city that is only deep below.

TO MY DAUGHTER

My dear one, years alone,
lost in the crowded attic
of childhood or face pressed
to widow's-watch glass while I
like a maddened Ahab pursued
the white, spume-blown hulk
through violent seas, or lesser
narwhales:
           I dreamt
I walked the shore, by death's-
wash roar, and a gray
house loomed, and one
in the garden there, young
woman lovely in sunlight,
with bright hair. "Daddy!"
you cried in welcoming joy,
but I knew. "Where's
your mother?" "In the house."
Warped clapboards and rotting
stoop, salt garden
picketed with whale bones.
"Where am I?" "Under
the sea." "I'm sorry I didn't
do well by you." "That's
all right. *We're* happy here."

My daughter, I shall wear
the one laughing face
in Hell, for love of you.

THE CRICKETS IN THEIR ANTIQUE
REAL WORLD

shrill Ethiops of the grassblade-cry,
and dustdrenched beetles clicking, and rasp
of fans where tobacco-rich grasshoppers fly
(though caterpillars climb by furry hunches
in silence to the ravel day), and dry
cornstalk scrape, and crows scaring
upward like scattershot peppering the sky,
and grackles and grackles and grackles in bunches
breaking southwards from their sparse branchberths
with a rinsing noise—the year's full
hull receding through highnoontide surf.

AN OLD MAN IN THE ORCHARD

at midmorning, knowledgeable,
a use of pruning shears.
The uncut grasses touch
his knees. His strawbrimmed
hat: an ordinary quietness.
Why am I so joyful?
Of course I think of bees,
fruit trees and bees
and sun on leaves. It is
the earth's fruitfulness. A bent
old man, and the limbs
sagging with globed oranges.

POEM PLAIN AS A STONE

I

The horses have been penned up
for the night. The dry cornstalks
crackle at their feet. In the halfdark
the dark forms move
and the white horse, negative
of my thoughts, noses chaff.
(How many times have I put
my hands in among bees,
on Langstroth's frames, and felt
the warmth there?) A night wind
shifts the leaves. I have worked
hard all day, my body
is heavy. Someone hollers
across a field. The tarred stones
of the roadside scatter from under
my feet.
                    —*Great black*
wings tighten, I am crowded
with terror, all stoppered, a silence
with the density of flesh
                              wellnigh
knocked to my knees like a beast
under a bludgeon.

II

                    The wings open
to a light greater than the combustion
of phosporus. Slowly the roots

of light spread out, then
with a rush out past all thought,
snap into crystal for they have touched
all things. I could weep but that
in the silence of eternity comes the horse
of joy. No hand
ever opened, no leaf
ever turned but opens and turns
now: in the pockets of time
a beetle is as great as I am,
equally blessed, and the innumerable
is one. I am suffused
with a peace more pervasive than blood.

III

The white horse has not moved
one step or touched
a splinter more of chaff.
He is pure light. I could wash
my hungry hands in his flesh.
His saddle sores are holy. The fly
that had buzzed in his mane all
afternoon and is hunched up now
to the heat of a barn rafter
dreams of the sacrament.

IV

                        The bus
to Grand Island, Nebraska,
roars by. The people in it
are bathed in a brown light.
Even in darkness we are linked
by light. We do not know
our own divinity. It is
the element we live in.

SONG, CRYSTAL RADIO SONG

Were you blue, girl, sixteen, 1924,
in bracelets, flat-breasted, apricot
dress, bobbed hair and false
furs?
      Alone in the room, wind
the Victrola. It was years before,
the moment you caught your sister,
breathless and laughing, sunlight
and the snowball bush. She was awkward,
easy to catch, hardly ever spoke.
Then in the parlor you both
listened to the song, the earphones
nested in a tin bowl. After lunch
they washed her face, braided
her hair, put her
in the new, blue dress you
had cried for the day before
and sent her to the asylum where
she was homesick nineteen years.

For you, *Cosmopolitan* love. Your
heart leapt, on the wedding night
was spasmodic with terror, flattened and thudded
in contracted labor: two plump
sons, the living room suite,
kitchen, radio, self-starting Ford.
Thelma
worked in the laundry, had her room
with its simple cot, wrote childish letters
and died.

94

Now, after sixty years,
dark trees rushing past,
Volkswagen headlights piercing the dark,
the song comes out of your mouth
like a new penny out of dark water.

SOMETIMES I THINK I AM AN
ELEMENTAL ANGEL

with all the ignorance that implies,
able to move into others' beings,
but with too much light, lacking
in pity. It is Puck's complaint,
pinching the barks of dogs to a higher
pitch, sleeping in the pockets of drunkards,
pestering lovers with the diligence of a flea.
The night of the moneylender's murder, when Geisel
without lantern or moonlight drove back
to his rescued farm by the roundabout way,
I sat on the terret ring of his horse
in absolute glee. I am there when the car
goes off the road and you crawl
out through a window and scream, "Is George
all right?" I am the blindfold deserter
at the post, the Jesuit in his cell, the Vietnamese
child coming toward you with the pulled
grenade.
            Compassion would kill me.

EVERGREENS DECK THE YEAR

in black and darker green
on the hill. Crows tell
what they will with laughter
or coughs across the snow.
Salt is on the roads.
It is the broken-hip time,
stripped willows and ribbed
deer. Here in a row
this natural fenceline, chopped
back to black scepters
in cold ermine—or fingerless
amputations, time-charred,
unwrapped from cruelest white
welted from wrist to wrist
with old barbed-wire and leads
us where we go. If one
wild stump jabs
a pliant antler at our hearts,
still we learn nothing,
nothing that we *want* to know.
O my dear kind,
what is there to know
except this starstorm snow
again, and that high on the hill
the mute, stepping grouse
under the very name of death
print the crust and peck needles
and make small breath?

DOGS COUNTLESS AS STARS

bark in the night. One pulses
like a small sun. Some
are in constellations, their energies
illuminate what would otherwise be
a silence deep as space.
    Those with the shortest, sharpest
glint are new beings. Others
. generate a more used and casual
scintillation. Their hearts are singular,
savage as the stars.
                     Outside
my window, on the other side
of the fence, a horse shifts
and blows, in the company of sleep,
and I am safe
                for one
                        more
moment in this house.

ABOUT THE AUTHOR

R. G. VLIET is the author of two previous collections of poems, *Events & Celebrations* (1966) and *The Man with the Black Mouth* (1970), as well as two novels. He has three times won the Texas Institute of Letters Award, twice for his books of poems and most recently for his novel *Solitudes* (1977). In 1968 he was a Rockefeller Foundation Fellow in Fiction and Poetry. "Vliet's writing," Malcolm Cowley has written, "is close to becoming a national treasure."

Mr. Vliet was educated in Texas and did graduate work at Yale. Son of a naval medical officer, he has lived in American Samoa (as a child), in the Southwest, New England, and Mexico. For the past eight years he and his wife have been working a small farmstead on a mountainside in Vermont. Mr. Vliet is currently at work on a third novel, to be published by Random House.